THIS BOOK BELONGS TO:

Illustrations by Piet Aukeman

Design by Hana Anouk Nakamura

ISBN: 978-1-4197-3255-3

© 2018 Abrams

Printed and bound in China

10 9 8 7 6

Abrams Noterie products are available at special discounts when
purchased in quantity for premiums and promotions as well as
fundraising or educational use. Special editions can also be created
to specification. For details, contact specialsales@abramsbooks.com
or the address below.

ABRAMS The Art of Books
195 Broadway, New York, NY 10007
abramsbooks.com

"A book, too, can be a star, 'explosive material, capable of stirring up fresh life endlessly,' a living fire to lighten the darkness, leading out into the expanding universe."

—Madeleine L'Engle

AT BOOK RIOT, we believe that reading for escape and entertainment is just as valid and just as important as reading to learn and grow, and there's room for books that do all of these things and more. Books make our world better, and they make it bigger, and there's no right or wrong way to be reader. If you love books and you're open to all the ways they might change you, you're already winning.

We created the Read Harder Challenge in 2015, with the belief that the books we read should be as diverse as readers are. We hear from readers all the time who want to read more broadly, to support writers whose voices haven't traditionally been heard, and to make their reading lives more reflective of their values, but they don't know where to start. That's where Read Harder and the challenges included in this journal come in.

The twelve challenges you'll find throughout this reading log are intended to inspire you to pick up books that represent experiences and places and cultures that might be different from your own. For every challenge, we've included five great recommendations to get you started, but feel free to do your own research about books that fit and go your own way. If you come across a title you want to save for later, add it to the To-Be-Read pile in the back of this journal!

Remember, Read Harder isn't about reading a bigger number of books or reading more difficult ones. It's about paying more attention to what you read and how you choose your books. It's about reading with purpose and intention. Use this journal as the jumping-off point of a new and exciting literary journey. We'll be here to cheer you on.

Thanks for joining the Read Harder party! We're excited you're here, and we hope you'll come see us at bookriot.com to continue the adventure.

Read on,

Team Book Riot

CHALLENGE CHECKLIST

READ:

◯ A BOOK ABOUT BOOKS

◯ A BOOK YOU WOULD NORMALLY CONSIDER
A GUILTY PLEASURE

◯ A BOOK ABOUT A CURRENT SOCIAL
OR POLITICAL ISSUE

◯ A BOOK THAT WAS ORIGINALLY PUBLISHED
IN ANOTHER LANGUAGE

◯ A BOOK WITH AN LGBTQ MAIN CHARACTER,
WRITTEN BY AN LGBTQ AUTHOR

◯ RE-READ A BOOK YOU READ IN SCHOOL

◯ AN AWARD-WINNING YOUNG ADULT BOOK

◯ A BOOK BY AN IMMIGRANT OR
WITH A CENTRAL IMMIGRATION NARRATIVE

◯ A COLLECTION OF SHORT STORIES

◯ A BOOK ABOUT SPACE

◯ A BOOK PUBLISHED BY AN INDEPENDENT PRESS

◯ A BOOK BY AN AUTHOR FROM ANOTHER CONTINENT

TITLE

AUTHOR

PUBLISHER:

YEAR PUBLISHED:

GENRE/SUBJECT:

STARTED

FINISHED

REVIEW:

This book in 3 words

-
-
-

RATING: A   B   C   D   F

NOTES, QUOTES, and other things to remember:

TITLE

AUTHOR

PUBLISHER:

YEAR PUBLISHED:

GENRE/SUBJECT:

STARTED

FINISHED

REVIEW:

This book in 3 words

-
-
-

RATING: **A**   **B**   **C**   **D**   **F**

NOTES, QUOTES, and other things to remember:

TITLE

AUTHOR

PUBLISHER:

YEAR PUBLISHED:

GENRE/SUBJECT:

STARTED

FINISHED

REVIEW:

This book in 3 words

-
-
-

RATING: A   B   C   D   F

NOTES, QUOTES, and other things to remember:

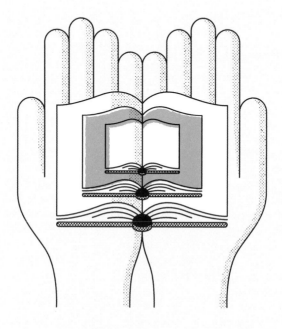

"She read books as one would breathe air, to fill up and live."

–Annie Dillard

CHALLENGE #1

Read a book about books.

The act of reading is solitary, but being a reader means sharing a common language with other people who love books and whose lives have been shaped by them. Reading gives us a window into other people's experiences and a new lens through which to make sense of our own, and reading about reading reminds us that we're not alone. James Baldwin put it this way: "You think your pain and your heartbreak are unprecedented in the history of the world, but then you read." It's really pretty magical when you think about it.

Books about books are so numerous and beloved that many bookstores set aside special sections for them. There's literary criticism, memoirs about reading, fiction set in bookstores and libraries, and on and on.

Use this challenge to consider what books and reading mean to you by reading about what they mean to someone else.

Here are some excellent books about books, written by bibliophiles, for bibliophiles.

The World Between Two Covers by **Ann Morgan**: Morgan documents how a project to read one book from every country in the world became a life-changing exploration of culture and identity, and demonstrated the value of reading outside your comfort zone. (Bonus: this book is packed with recommendations for books translated into English, if you're looking for more picks to help you with Challenge #4.)

What We See When We Read by **Peter Mendelsund**: In this beautifully illustrated, brain-bending work, Random House book designer Mendelsund investigates how words on the page become images in our heads as we read. This isn't about neurology, it's about visualization and what it feels like when we see stories in our minds.

Reading Lolita in Tehran: A Memoir in Books by **Azar Nafisi**: Literature professor Nafisi recounts the secret weekly meetings she held with seven female students in the Islamic Republic of Iran over the course of two years, during which they read and discussed banned Western classics.

84, Charing Cross Road by **Helene Hanff**: Oozing with charm and bookish asides, this collection of twenty years of correspondence between Hanff, a freelance writer in New York, and a used-book dealer she befriends in London, is bound to delight.

A Reader on Reading by **Alberto Manguel**: The man once described as "the Casanova of reading" contends that the act of reading and the search for narrative are the defining features of the human species.

TITLE

AUTHOR

PUBLISHER:

YEAR PUBLISHED:

GENRE/SUBJECT:

STARTED

FINISHED

REVIEW:

This book in 3 words

-
-
-

RATING: **A**   **B**   **C**   **D**   **F**

NOTES, QUOTES, and other things to remember:

AFTERTHOUGHTS

How did this challenge influence your reading experience?

_____

_____

_____

_____

_____

_____

_____

What insights did you gain from this challenge?

_____

_____

_____

_____

_____

_____

_____

_____

TITLE

AUTHOR

PUBLISHER:

YEAR PUBLISHED:

GENRE/SUBJECT:

STARTED **FINISHED**

REVIEW:

_____

_____

_____

_____

_____

_____

_____

_____

This book in 3 words

-
-
-

RATING: **A** **B** **C** **D** **F**

NOTES, QUOTES, and other things to remember:

TITLE

AUTHOR

PUBLISHER:

YEAR PUBLISHED:

GENRE/SUBJECT:

STARTED

FINISHED

REVIEW:

This book in 3 words

-
-
-

RATING: A   B   C   D   F

NOTES, QUOTES, and other things to remember:

TITLE

AUTHOR

PUBLISHER:

YEAR PUBLISHED:

GENRE/SUBJECT:

STARTED

FINISHED

REVIEW:

This book in 3 words

-
-
-

RATING: A   B   C   D   F

NOTES, QUOTES, and other things to remember:

"Love what you love."

–Ray Bradbury

CHALLENGE #2

Read a book you would normally consider a guilty pleasure.

Somewhere along the way in our reading lives, many of us pick up the idea that some kinds of books are more worthy, valuable, or legitimate than others. We begin to believe that there's "Real Reading", and then there's "Secret Fun Reading", and that we should be proud of the former and quietly embarrassed by the latter. Remember when reading was just for pleasure, just for pure enjoyment? What happened?

Maybe you abandoned a beloved genre altogether because it didn't feel serious enough. Maybe you thought you had to read differently in order to seem as smart or as sophisticated as the people around you. Or maybe it has simply been too long since you read something because you *wanted to*, not because you felt like you *should*. Never feel guilty for enjoying what you read and reading what you enjoy.

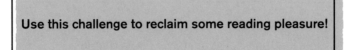

Use this challenge to reclaim some reading pleasure!

Here are some great reads in genres frequently cited as guilty pleasures.

A Rogue by Any Other Name by **Sarah MacLean** (romance): Come for the punny titles, stay for the smart, self-determined heroines in this Regency romance with a decidedly modern perspective.

When Dimple Met Rishi by **Sandhya Menon** (young adult): Opposites attract in this YA rom-com about teen coders whose parents' attempts to arrange their marriage go delightfully awry.

Is Everyone Hanging Out Without Me? by **Mindy Kaling** (celebrity memoir): The comedian, actress, and writer's whip-smart humor is on full display in these essays that range from her childhood and early career to dating angst, friendships, and fashion.

The Fifth Season by **N.K. Jemisin** (fantasy): This 2016 winner of the Hugo Award has fantastic world building, an amazing magic system, and a badass, middle-aged heroine who wields the most powerful skills in the world.

Saga by **Brian K. Vaughan** and **Fiona Staples** (comics): *Romeo and Juliet* meets Star Wars with a bizarre but wonderful cast of characters, including bounty hunters with lie-detecting cats, cybernetic monarchs, and teenage ghosts.

TITLE

AUTHOR

PUBLISHER:

YEAR PUBLISHED:

GENRE/SUBJECT:

STARTED

FINISHED

REVIEW:

This book in 3 words

-
-
-

RATING: A B C D F

NOTES, QUOTES, and other things to remember:

AFTERTHOUGHTS

How did this challenge influence your reading experience?

_____

_____

_____

_____

_____

_____

_____

What insights did you gain from this challenge?

_____

_____

_____

_____

_____

_____

_____

_____

TITLE

AUTHOR

PUBLISHER:

YEAR PUBLISHED:

GENRE/SUBJECT:

STARTED

FINISHED

REVIEW:

This book in 3 words

-
-
-

RATING: A   B   C   D   F

NOTES, QUOTES, and other things to remember:

_____

_____

_____

_____

_____

_____

_____

_____

_____

_____

_____

_____

_____

_____

_____

_____

_____

_____

_____

_____

_____

_____

TITLE

AUTHOR

PUBLISHER:

YEAR PUBLISHED:

GENRE/SUBJECT:

STARTED   **FINISHED**

REVIEW:

This book in 3 words

-
-
-

RATING: **A**   **B**   **C**   **D**   **F**

NOTES, QUOTES, and other things to remember:

TITLE

AUTHOR

PUBLISHER:

YEAR PUBLISHED:

GENRE/SUBJECT:

STARTED　　　　　　**FINISHED**

REVIEW:

This book in 3 words

-
-
-

RATING:　　**A**　　**B**　　**C**　　**D**　　**F**

NOTES, QUOTES, and other things to remember:

"Let us pick up our books and our pens, they are the most powerful weapons."

–Malala Yousafzai

CHALLENGE #3

Read a book about a current social or political issue.

The old rule about not talking politics or religion might work for dinner parties, but it shouldn't apply to the bookshelf. The world is a complicated, messy, often contradictory place, and the internet gives us access to ideas and arguments from all corners. It's more important than ever to know not just *what* you think, but *why*.

Reading about current social and political events serves the dual purpose of expanding your awareness to clarify your own thinking and enabling you to discuss and defend it more effectively.

Use this challenge to read deeply about an issue you might be more accustomed to encountering in tweets and sound bites.

Here are some outstanding reads about the biggest issues of the day.

Tears We Cannot Stop: A Sermon to White America by **Michael Eric Dyson**: Distinguished sociology professor, writer, and minister, Dyson writes an impassioned, important letter to white Americans explaining white privilege and urging them to face difficult truths about America's racist history in order to move forward.

On Immunity: An Inoculation by **Eula Biss**: Following the birth of her first child, Biss found herself surrounded by conflicting ideas and arguments about vaccinations. Here, she works to separate the facts from her feelings and make the vaccination question less about personal preference and more about social responsibility.

Bread, Wine, Chocolate: The Slow Loss of Foods We Love by **Simran Sethi**: In this examination of monocultures and the dangers of an increasingly standardized diet, journalist Simran Sethi explores the cultural importance of certain foods and how we are in danger of losing them.

Incarceration Nations: A Journey to Justice in Prisons Around the World by **Baz Dreisinger**: After visiting prisons around the world, Dreisinger, a professor, journalist, and founder of the Prison-to-College-Pipeline, presents the lessons she learned and the human stories of incarcerated men and women and those who imprison them.

Feminism Is for Everybody by **bell hooks**: This modern classic provides a thorough introduction to feminism and how it is connected to eliminating all oppressions.

TITLE

AUTHOR

PUBLISHER:

YEAR PUBLISHED:

GENRE/SUBJECT:

STARTED

FINISHED

REVIEW:

This book in 3 words

-
-
-

RATING: **A**   **B**   **C**   **D**   **F**

NOTES, QUOTES, and other things to remember:

AFTERTHOUGHTS

How did this challenge influence your reading experience?

_____

_____

_____

_____

_____

_____

_____

What insights did you gain from this challenge?

_____

_____

_____

_____

_____

_____

_____

_____

TITLE

AUTHOR

PUBLISHER:

YEAR PUBLISHED:

GENRE/SUBJECT:

STARTED   **FINISHED**

REVIEW:

_____

_____

_____

_____

_____

_____

_____

_____

This book in 3 words

-
-
-

RATING: **A**   **B**   **C**   **D**   **F**

NOTES, QUOTES, and other things to remember:

TITLE

AUTHOR

PUBLISHER:

YEAR PUBLISHED:

GENRE/SUBJECT:

STARTED

FINISHED

REVIEW:

This book in 3 words

-
-
-

RATING:　　A　　B　　C　　D　　F

NOTES, QUOTES, and other things to remember:

TITLE

AUTHOR

PUBLISHER:

YEAR PUBLISHED:

GENRE/SUBJECT:

STARTED   **FINISHED**

REVIEW:

_____

_____

_____

_____

_____

_____

_____

_____

This book in 3 words

-
-
-

RATING: A   B   C   D   F

NOTES, QUOTES, and other things to remember:

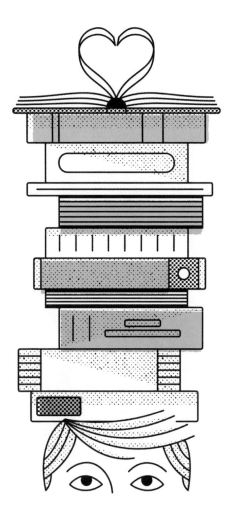

"If you talk to a man in a language he understands, that goes to his head. If you talk to him in his language, that goes to his heart."

—Nelson Mandela

CHALLENGE #4

Read a book that was originally published in another language.

The idea of reading literature in translation strikes fear into the hearts of many readers. Books written in other languages are, by definition, foreign. They may describe cultures we're not familiar with, contain references and jokes we've never heard before, and ask us to place ourselves squarely into lives we've never imagined. It can be unsettling and more than a little intimidating.

But reading translated work can also be the very best kind of magic: a window into previously unknown experiences and a reminder that so much of the human experience is universal.

Use this challenge to remind yourself that great books come in all languages.

Here's a variety of books originally published in languages other than English.

Out by **Natsuo Kirino** (Japanese): If *Fried Green Tomatoes* and *Gone Girl* had a really dangerous baby, it would be this electrifying revenge thriller.

The Alchemist by **Paulo Coelho** (Portuguese): This inspiring tale about an Andalusian shepherd boy, often cited as a life-changing read, is ultimately about learning to follow to your heart and find happiness wherever life takes you.

The Queue by **Basma Abdel Aziz** (Arabic): Longlisted for the 2017 Best Translated Book Award, this is a surreal look at the absurdity and irrationality of totalitarian government.

A Novel Bookstore by **Laurence Cossé** (French): People connected to the Good Novel bookstore in Paris keep turning up dead, and the only thing they have in common is their taste in books.

Kingdom Cons by **Yuri Herrera** (Spanish): Considered by many to be Mexico's greatest contemporary novelist, Herrera mixes surrealism, fables, and romance in this genre-bending crime novel.

TITLE

AUTHOR

PUBLISHER:

YEAR PUBLISHED:

GENRE/SUBJECT:

STARTED | **FINISHED**

REVIEW:

_____

_____

_____

_____

_____

_____

_____

_____

This book in 3 words

-
-
-

RATING: **A**   **B**   **C**   **D**   **F**

NOTES, QUOTES, and other things to remember:

AFTERTHOUGHTS

How did this challenge influence your reading experience?

_____

_____

_____

_____

_____

_____

_____

What insights did you gain from this challenge?

_____

_____

_____

_____

_____

_____

_____

TITLE

AUTHOR

PUBLISHER:

YEAR PUBLISHED:

GENRE/SUBJECT:

STARTED   **FINISHED**

REVIEW:

_____

_____

_____

_____

_____

_____

_____

_____

This book in 3 words

-
-
-

RATING: **A**   **B**   **C**   **D**   **F**

NOTES, QUOTES, and other things to remember:

TITLE

AUTHOR

PUBLISHER:

YEAR PUBLISHED:

GENRE/SUBJECT:

STARTED   **FINISHED**

REVIEW:

This book in 3 words

-
-
-

RATING: A   B   C   D   F

NOTES, QUOTES, and other things to remember:

_____

_____

_____

_____

_____

_____

_____

_____

_____

_____

_____

_____

_____

_____

_____

_____

_____

_____

_____

_____

_____

TITLE

AUTHOR

PUBLISHER:

YEAR PUBLISHED:

GENRE/SUBJECT:

STARTED

FINISHED

REVIEW:

This book in 3 words

-
-
-

RATING: A   B   C   D   F

NOTES, QUOTES, and other things to remember:

"Love is love is love."

–Lin-Manuel Miranda

Read a book with an LGBTQ main character, written by an LGBTQ author.

Recently, there's been a real push in the reader community for books that acknowledge the diversity of human experiences and identities. (For more on this, check out weneeddiversebooks.org.) Despite the progress that has been made, every year's list of the most frequently banned and challenged books contains many titles featuring LGBTQ themes.

No one is more qualified to tell stories about being LGBTQ than members of the community themselves, and that's why this challenge isn't just to read a story with an LGBTQ main character but to find one that is told by someone who speaks from the authority of personal experience.

Use this challenge to read a book that celebrates love, and shows there are great stories to be told from every point of view

Here are some books written from the LGBTQ perspective:

Here Comes the Sun by **Nicole Dennis-Benn**: Written with an intimate knowledge and understanding of Jamaica, this novel shows the seedier side of paradise, exploring queerness, race, religion, and education through the story of a mother and her two daughters struggling to make a better life for themselves.

Kissing the Witch by **Emma Donoghue**: This collection of feminist, mostly-lesbian retellings of fairy tales by the author of Room has become something of a classic, and when you read it, you'll know why.

If I Was Your Girl by **Meredith Russo**: Follow Amanda Hardy, a trans teen girl, as she moves to a small school in rural Tennessee and navigates social cliques, new friendships, and a major crush.

Aristotle and Dante Discover the Secrets of the Universe by **Benjamin Alire Saenz**: It takes two summers to figure things out, but Ari makes the difficult transition from having no friends to having a best friend (Dante), to realizing that he is in love with that best friend. But what to do? (Bonus: Lin-Manuel Miranda reads the audiobook!)

The Gap of Time by **Jeanette Winterson**: Reimagining Shakespeare's *The Winter's Tale*, Winterson moves the story to London just after the financial crisis and a storm-ravaged American South. With flawed characters entangled in jealousy, obsession, and even self-delusion, don't be surprised when no one escapes unscathed.

TITLE

AUTHOR

PUBLISHER:

YEAR PUBLISHED:

GENRE/SUBJECT:

STARTED   **FINISHED**

REVIEW:

This book in 3 words

-
-
-

RATING: **A**   **B**   **C**   **D**   **F**

NOTES, QUOTES, and other things to remember:

AFTERTHOUGHTS

How did this challenge influence your reading experience?

_____

_____

_____

_____

_____

_____

_____

What insights did you gain from this challenge?

_____

_____

_____

_____

_____

_____

_____

TITLE

AUTHOR

PUBLISHER:

YEAR PUBLISHED:

GENRE/SUBJECT:

STARTED   **FINISHED**

REVIEW:

This book in 3 words

-
-
-

RATING: A   B   C   D   F

NOTES, QUOTES, and other things to remember:

TITLE

AUTHOR

PUBLISHER:

YEAR PUBLISHED:

GENRE/SUBJECT:

STARTED   **FINISHED**

REVIEW:

This book in 3 words

-
-
-

RATING: **A**   **B**   **C**   **D**   **F**

NOTES, QUOTES, and other things to remember:

TITLE

AUTHOR

PUBLISHER:

YEAR PUBLISHED:

GENRE/SUBJECT:

STARTED   **FINISHED**

REVIEW:

This book in 3 words

RATING: A   B   C   D   F

NOTES, QUOTES, and other things to remember:

"Once you learn to read, you will be forever free."

—Frederick Douglass

CHALLENGE #6

Re-read a book you read in school.

Whether you loved school or hated it, there's probably at least one book you were assigned to read that you think about once in a while. Maybe the book made a huge impression on you at the time, or maybe you felt like you didn't quite "get it" and you want to give it another go. Now that you're older (and maybe wiser), is there a story you might understand in a new way or a challenging literary structure that would be more fun now without the pressure of a deadline or a test?

However long ago your first reading was, while the book will be the same when you go back to it, *you* will be different, and that's what makes re-reading so interesting!

Use this challenge to return to a book you've read before and reflect on how you have changed since the first time around.

Here are some of the greatest hits from school syllabi to get you going.

To Kill a Mockingbird by **Harper Lee**: Americans often cite this 1960s classic about racism and life in a small southern town as their favorite novel. A lot about American life has changed since it was written, but a lot has stayed the same. Return to it with fresh eyes and reexamine your nostalgia.

Beloved by **Toni Morrison**: The most important novel from Nobel Laureate Morrison is also the most daunting and, frankly, too complex for most teenagers. If you struggled with it in school, take a deep breath and dive back in. And if you loved it then, you're bound to find even more to love the second time around.

One Hundred Years of Solitude by **Gabriel García Márquez**: Strange things happen in this landmark work of magical realism. It can be a fantastic read if you're willing to be a little unsettled, and that openness to the unfamiliar comes with time and age. See how well you can hang with Garcia Marquez's style now.

1984 by **George Orwell**: Orwell's dystopian political novel became a best-seller again in early 2017, sixty-eight years after its original publication. How does living in today's world affect your reading of a cautionary tale from 1949?

Pride and Prejudice by **Jane Austen**: It is a truth universally acknowledged that there's more going on in this Regency romance than first meets the eye. Find new depths in a beloved story with the benefit of age and wisdom.

TITLE

AUTHOR

PUBLISHER:

YEAR PUBLISHED:

GENRE/SUBJECT:

STARTED

FINISHED

REVIEW:

This book in 3 words

-
-
-

RATING: A B C D F

NOTES, QUOTES, and other things to remember:

AFTERTHOUGHTS

How did this challenge influence your reading experience?

_____

_____

_____

_____

_____

_____

_____

What insights did you gain from this challenge?

_____

_____

_____

_____

_____

_____

_____

_____

TITLE

AUTHOR

PUBLISHER:

YEAR PUBLISHED:

GENRE/SUBJECT:

STARTED

FINISHED

REVIEW:

This book in 3 words

-
-
-

RATING: A B C D F

NOTES, QUOTES, and other things to remember:

TITLE

AUTHOR

PUBLISHER:

YEAR PUBLISHED:

GENRE/SUBJECT:

STARTED | **FINISHED**

REVIEW:

_____

_____

_____

_____

_____

_____

_____

_____

This book in 3 words

-
-
-

RATING: **A**   **B**   **C**   **D**   **F**

NOTES, QUOTES, and other things to remember:

TITLE

AUTHOR

PUBLISHER:

YEAR PUBLISHED:

GENRE/SUBJECT:

STARTED

FINISHED

REVIEW:

This book in 3 words

-
-
-

RATING: A B C D F

NOTES, QUOTES, and other things to remember:

"I want to write for readers who can perform miracles. Only children perform miracles when they read."

—Astrid Lindgren

CHALLENGE #7

Read an award-winning young adult book.

Whether you just graduated into adulthood or left your teen years behind several decades ago, chances are the memories of your own adolescence remain sharp in your mind. And that's why young adult books aren't just for young adults: Because growing up is something we all have to do.

Just like the characters in adult fiction, the heroes in YA books aren't perfect. They make mistakes and bad decisions, and bad things do happen to them. But they're also smart enough or kind enough or brave enough to do the right thing—the *hard* thing—when it counts the most. Great young adult books connect us to something essential and true that resonates regardless of our age.

Use this challenge to get acquainted (or reacquainted) with what being young tells us about being human.

Here are some exciting reads for both long-time YA fans and newbies.

If You Could Be Mine by **Sara Farizan**: Seventeen-year-old Sahar has been in love with her best friend, Nasrin, since they were six. But Iran is a dangerous place for two girls in love, so they carry on in secret—until Nasrin's parents announce that they've arranged her marriage . . .

Yaqui Delgado Wants to Kick Your Ass by **Meg Medina**: When Piddy moves to a new school, she learns that a girl named Yaqui wants to beat her up, but she never finds out why. This is a novel not only about bullying, but also about family, grief, and friendship.

Bone Gap by **Laura Ruby**: People are known to just disappear from Bone Gap, but Finn O'Sullivan knows that Roza was actually kidnapped by a man he can't remember. The problem is, the searches never turned up anything and no one believes him. So what really happened to Roza?

March by **John Lewis, Andrew Aydin, and Nate Powell**: In this graphic novel trilogy, Congressman John Lewis documents the commitment to justice and nonviolence that has taken him from a segregated schoolroom to the halls of Congress, and from receiving beatings from state troopers to receiving the Medal of Freedom from the first African-American president.

The Absolutely True Diary of a Part-Time Indian by **Sherman Alexie**: Teenager Arnold Spirit, aka Junior, is growing up on the Spokane Indian Reservation. When he leaves the reservation school to attend a predominantly white school nearby, he discovers it may be harder than he imagined to make a new life and create a new identity for himself.

TITLE

AUTHOR

PUBLISHER:

YEAR PUBLISHED:

GENRE/SUBJECT:

STARTED

FINISHED

REVIEW:

This book in 3 words

-
-
-

RATING: A   B   C   D   F

NOTES, QUOTES, and other things to remember:

AFTERTHOUGHTS

How did this challenge influence your reading experience?

_____

_____

_____

_____

_____

_____

_____

_____

What insights did you gain from this challenge?

_____

_____

_____

_____

_____

_____

_____

_____

_____

_____

TITLE

AUTHOR

PUBLISHER:

YEAR PUBLISHED:

GENRE/SUBJECT:

STARTED   **FINISHED**

REVIEW:

This book in 3 words

-
-
-

RATING: **A**   **B**   **C**   **D**   **F**

NOTES, QUOTES, and other things to remember:

TITLE

AUTHOR

PUBLISHER:

YEAR PUBLISHED:

GENRE/SUBJECT:

STARTED

FINISHED

REVIEW:

This book in 3 words

-
-
-

RATING: A   B   C   D   F

NOTES, QUOTES, and other things to remember:

_____

_____

_____

_____

_____

_____

_____

_____

_____

_____

_____

_____

_____

_____

_____

_____

_____

_____

_____

_____

_____

_____

_____

_____

TITLE

AUTHOR

PUBLISHER:

YEAR PUBLISHED:

GENRE/SUBJECT:

STARTED   **FINISHED**

REVIEW:

This book in 3 words

-
-
-

RATING: A   B   C   D   F

NOTES, QUOTES, and other things to remember:

*"No one leaves home unless
home is the mouth of a shark."*

–Warsan Shire

CHALLENGE #8

Read a book by an immigrant or with a central immigration narrative.

You might have heard it said that there are only two plots in all of literature: A person goes on a journey, or a stranger comes to town. Books about the immigrant experience give you both of these plots in one place, examining what it means to leave home and strike out for someplace new and also showing what it is like to be the stranger who comes to town. More importantly, these stories ask and answer the question of why someone would leave their home country and all that is familiar to start over in a foreign place, often with very few resources.

The lived reality of giving up everything in hopes of building something new and better is the stuff that great novels are made of.

Use this challenge to think about your perception of immigrants and immigration and try to read beyond those lines.

Here are some first-rate reads by and about immigrants and immigrant experiences.

The Book of Unknown Americans by **Cristina Henríquez:** Two immigrant families (one from Mexico and one from Panama) who have come to the U.S. for different reasons find their paths colliding as their teen daughter and son get to know each other.

Behold the Dreamers by **Imbolo Mbue**: Exploring the American Dream from two sides, this novel is about Cameroonian immigrants living in Harlem and the wealthy Lehman Brothers executives they work for just as the economy starts to crash in 2008.

In the Country We Love by **Diane Guerrero**: The star of *Jane the Virgin* and *Orange is the New Black* documents the reality of being undocumented in the U.S. and recounts how she found herself completely alone at age fourteen, having slipped through the cracks of the system that deported her family.

The Namesake by **Jhumpa Lahiri**: This novel follows a family from Calcutta as they make sense of their new lives in Cambridge, Massachusetts, with special focus on their son, who grows up straddling two cultures.

Funny in Farsi by **Firoozeh Dumas**: In this hilarious and thoughtful memoir, Dumas, whose family moved from Iran to southern California when she was seven, shares challenges, triumphs, and memorable moments of navigating American culture.

TITLE

AUTHOR

PUBLISHER:

YEAR PUBLISHED:

GENRE/SUBJECT:

STARTED

FINISHED

REVIEW:

This book in 3 words

-
-
-

RATING: **A** **B** **C** **D** **F**

NOTES, QUOTES, and other things to remember:

AFTERTHOUGHTS

How did this challenge influence your reading experience?

_____

_____

_____

_____

_____

_____

_____

_____

What insights did you gain from this challenge?

_____

_____

_____

_____

_____

_____

_____

_____

_____

TITLE

AUTHOR

PUBLISHER:

YEAR PUBLISHED:

GENRE/SUBJECT:

STARTED

FINISHED

REVIEW:

This book in 3 words

- •
- •
- •

RATING: **A**   **B**   **C**   **D**   **F**

NOTES, QUOTES, and other things to remember:

TITLE

AUTHOR

PUBLISHER:

YEAR PUBLISHED:

GENRE/SUBJECT:

STARTED

FINISHED

REVIEW:

This book in 3 words

-
-
-

RATING: A   B   C   D   F

NOTES, QUOTES, and other things to remember:

_____

_____

_____

_____

_____

_____

_____

_____

_____

_____

_____

_____

_____

_____

_____

_____

_____

_____

_____

_____

_____

_____

TITLE

AUTHOR

PUBLISHER:

YEAR PUBLISHED:

GENRE/SUBJECT:

STARTED

FINISHED

REVIEW:

This book in 3 words

-
-
-

RATING: A   B   C   D   F

NOTES, QUOTES, and other things to remember:

"Great things are done by a series of small things brought together."

–Vincent van Gogh

Read a collection of short stories.

Ask any bookseller, and they'll tell you they meet a lot of readers who love fiction but don't have much experience with short stories. Most readers are more familiar with novels, but there's room for both in a robust reading life. As master short story writer Lorrie Moore said, "A short story is a love affair, a novel is a marriage. A short story is a photograph; a novel is a film."

Short stories are a wonderful way to pass a few minutes when you're waiting for the train or the bus, and they provide a satisfying means of keeping some reading time in your life when you can't fully commit to a novel. Together in a collection, short stories can link up to a larger theme, offer readers numerous new worlds and experiences to explore, and—in the very best ones—leave you with a sense that the whole is greater than the sum of its parts.

Use this challenge to explore new reading experiences with a collection of short stories.

Here's an array of excellent short story collections to get you started.

What It Means When a Man Falls From the Sky: Stories by **Lesley Nneka Arimah**: Every now and then, you find a debut so accomplished that it feels like it can't possibly be the writer's first book. This collection, which elegantly blends fable, mythology, and tales grounded firmly in real life, all told in evocative, unforgettable language, is one of them.

Children of the New World by **Alexander Weinstein**: Advances in technology lead to all kinds of trouble in these near-future dystopian stories, perfect for fans of *Black Mirror* and *Westworld*.

Ghost Summer by **Tananarive Due**: Horror fans, this one's for you! The stories in this collection aren't all about ghosts, but they are all creepy, haunting, and perfectly chilling against their sultry southern Florida setting.

Single, Carefree, Mellow by **Katherine Heiny**: If *Sex and the City* had a younger, smarter sister, it would be this collection of stories about the hilarities and humiliations modern women face in dating, sex, and relationships.

I Was a Revolutionary by **Andrew Malan Milward**: In this fascinating collection, Milward, a protégé of Marilynne Robinson and Tim O'Brien, weaves history book anecdotes set in and around Lawrence, Kansas, into something human, raw, and immediate.

TITLE

AUTHOR

PUBLISHER:

YEAR PUBLISHED:

GENRE/SUBJECT:

STARTED

FINISHED

REVIEW:

This book in 3 words

-
-
-

RATING: A   B   C   D   F

NOTES, QUOTES, and other things to remember:

AFTERTHOUGHTS

How did this challenge influence your reading experience?

_____

_____

_____

_____

_____

_____

_____

What insights did you gain from this challenge?

_____

_____

_____

_____

_____

_____

_____

TITLE

AUTHOR

PUBLISHER:

YEAR PUBLISHED:

GENRE/SUBJECT:

STARTED   **FINISHED**

REVIEW:

This book in 3 words

-
-
-

RATING: **A**   **B**   **C**   **D**   **F**

NOTES, QUOTES, and other things to remember:

TITLE

AUTHOR

PUBLISHER:

YEAR PUBLISHED:

GENRE/SUBJECT:

STARTED

FINISHED

REVIEW:

This book in 3 words

-
-
-

RATING: A   B   C   D   F

NOTES, QUOTES, and other things to remember:

TITLE

AUTHOR

PUBLISHER:

YEAR PUBLISHED:

GENRE/SUBJECT:

STARTED

FINISHED

REVIEW:

This book in 3 words

-
-
-

RATING: A   B   C   D   F

NOTES, QUOTES, and other things to remember:

"Never be limited by other people's limited imaginations."

–Mae Jemison

CHALLENGE #10

Read a book about space.

Long before Star Trek proposed "to boldly go where no man had gone before" or Neil Armstrong took "one small step for man, one giant leap for mankind," humans have been fascinated by outer space. The people of ancient civilizations turned their imaginations towards the heavens and created myths to explain celestial phenomena we still don't fully understand to this day. Browse any modern bookstore and you'll find shelves of amazing stories about the stars and space travel—both real and imagined.

If taking a step back can give you a new take on things, traveling to another planet or the far reaches of the galaxy or even a whole new universe can really make a difference.

Use this challenge to reach for the stars and fire up your sense of wonder.

Here are a few books that will take you out of this world.

Defy the Stars by **Claudia Gray**: Noemi and Abel are forced to work together despite their very different life-and-death priorities. Set in the vastness of space but firmly grounded in humanity, their not-quite-love story unravels against war, ethical questions around artificial intelligence, and what lies at the core of being human.

Stories of Your Life and Others by **Ted Chiang**: Automatons, aliens, and high-stakes questions abound in this collection of stories, which includes the tale that inspired the blockbuster film *Arrival*.

An Astronaut's Guide to Life on Earth by **Chris Hadfield**: In warm, humor-filled prose, Hadfield, one of the most experienced astronauts in the world, shares what going to space taught him about ingenuity, determination, and being prepared for anything.

Hidden Figures: The American Dream and the Untold Story of the Black Women Mathematicians Who Helped Win the Space Race by **Margot Lee Shetterly**: At a time when complex math problems were still done by humans wielding pencils and black Americans were still struggling with segregation, an exclusive and previously unrecognized group of brilliant black women cracked the equations that would enable the U.S. to send men into space.

The Martian by **Andy Weir**: Mark Watney is stranded on Mars after his crewmates, who think he's already dead, make an emergency evacuation. Can NASA find a way to get him home, and first, keep him alive long enough to see his rescuers arrive?

TITLE

AUTHOR

PUBLISHER:

YEAR PUBLISHED:

GENRE/SUBJECT:

STARTED   **FINISHED**

REVIEW:

_____

_____

_____

_____

_____

_____

_____

_____

This book in 3 words

-
-
-

RATING: A   B   C   D   F

NOTES, QUOTES, and other things to remember:

AFTERTHOUGHTS

How did this challenge influence your reading experience?

_____

_____

_____

_____

_____

_____

_____

What insights did you gain from this challenge?

_____

_____

_____

_____

_____

_____

_____

_____

TITLE

AUTHOR

PUBLISHER:

YEAR PUBLISHED:

GENRE/SUBJECT:

STARTED   **FINISHED**

REVIEW:

_____

_____

_____

_____

_____

_____

_____

_____

This book in 3 words

-
-
-

RATING: **A**   **B**   **C**   **D**   **F**

NOTES, QUOTES, and other things to remember:

TITLE

AUTHOR

PUBLISHER:

YEAR PUBLISHED:

GENRE/SUBJECT:

STARTED   **FINISHED**

REVIEW:

This book in 3 words

RATING: A   B   C   D   F

NOTES, QUOTES, and other things to remember:

TITLE

AUTHOR

PUBLISHER:

YEAR PUBLISHED:

GENRE/SUBJECT:

STARTED   **FINISHED**

REVIEW:

_____

_____

_____

_____

_____

_____

_____

_____

This book in 3 words

-
-
-

RATING: **A**   **B**   **C**   **D**   **F**

NOTES, QUOTES, and other things to remember:

"*The most courageous act is still to think for yourself.
Aloud.*"

—Coco Chanel

CHALLENGE #11

Read a book published by an independent press.

Bestseller rankings, book club lists, and round-ups of the latest books to be adapted for the big screen are all terrific ways to find your next read, and it's certainly fun to know what all the current buzz is about, but the big-name books aren't the whole story. While you can have a fun and fulfilling reading life stocking your shelves with titles from the mainstream publishers—the ones you're most likely to see reviewed in the media, and featured by major book retailers—you can take it to a whole other level with just a little digging.

For every Big Publisher, there are dozens of smaller independent presses putting out all kinds of amazing books. And what they may lack in marketing budget, they make up for in freedom to explore, experiment, and champion writers who just might be the next big thing.

Use this challenge to discover a book from an indie press you probably wouldn't have found on your own.

Here are five independent titles to help you start the journey.

We Show What We Have Learned and Other Stories by **Clare Beams** (Lookout Books): The stories in this delightfully strange debut collection are perfect for fans of Karen Russell and George Saunders. Get ready to get weird.

Juliet Takes a Breath by **Gabby Rivera** (Riverdale Avenue Books): Now that Juliet has come out to her parents, she has a plan: move to Portland, intern for a famous author, and figure out what being a Puerto Rican lesbian is all about.

A Murder in Time by **Julie McElwain** (Pegasus Books): Accidental time travel lands a modern-day FBI agent in a British castle in 1815, where she must catch a serial killer before he catches her.

Invisible Man Got the Whole World Watching by **Mychal Denzel Smith** (Nation Books): A young black man chronicles his political awakening and understanding of feminism, masculinity, LGBTQ issues, and what it means to be black in contemporary America.

I'll Tell You in Person by **Chloe Caldwell** (Coffee House Press): Here's a hilarious—and hilariously candid—collection of essays about failing, flailing, and frantically scrambling through a quarter-life crisis.

TITLE

AUTHOR

PUBLISHER:

YEAR PUBLISHED:

GENRE/SUBJECT:

STARTED

FINISHED

REVIEW:

This book in 3 words

RATING: A   B   C   D   F

NOTES, QUOTES, and other things to remember:

AFTERTHOUGHTS

How did this challenge influence your reading experience?

_____

_____

_____

_____

_____

_____

_____

_____

What insights did you gain from this challenge?

_____

_____

_____

_____

_____

_____

_____

_____

TITLE

AUTHOR

PUBLISHER:

YEAR PUBLISHED:

GENRE/SUBJECT:

STARTED

FINISHED

REVIEW:

This book in 3 words

RATING: A   B   C   D   F

NOTES, QUOTES, and other things to remember:

TITLE

AUTHOR

PUBLISHER:

YEAR PUBLISHED:

GENRE/SUBJECT:

STARTED   **FINISHED**

REVIEW:

This book in 3 words

-
-
-

RATING: **A**   **B**   **C**   **D**   **F**

NOTES, QUOTES, and other things to remember:

TITLE

AUTHOR

PUBLISHER:

YEAR PUBLISHED:

GENRE/SUBJECT:

STARTED

FINISHED

REVIEW:

This book in 3 words

-
-
-

RATING: A   B   C   D   F

NOTES, QUOTES, and other things to remember:

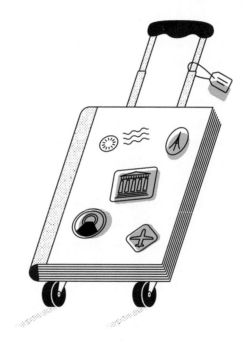

"Wherever you go becomes a part of you somehow."

—Anita Desai

CHALLENGE #12

Read a book by an author from another continent.

The places we live and languages we speak shape our thoughts and perceptions of the world. Universal experiences like coming of age, dealing with family complications, and making sense of where you fit in the big picture take on unique colors and textures depending on the setting. So, it follows that reading books written by people from other continents brings not just a change in geography but a shift in perspective.

LeVar Burton's *Reading Rainbow* theme song says that with a book, "I can go anywhere," and that's what this challenge is all about.

Use this challenge to expand your literary horizons, and maybe see your own corner of the world in a new light.

Here are five books that span the globe:

The Fishermen by **Chigozie Obioma** (Africa): This story follows the disintegration of a family in a small city in Nigeria, focusing on a group of brothers whose brutal cleaving drives and haunts the plot. Obioma has a remarkable ability to transform the most astounding events of youth into believable moments of personal growth, familial pain, and utter joy.

Inside Out and Back Again by **Thanhha Lai** (Asia): Told in verse from a child's perspective, this coming-of-age debut novel was inspired by the author's experience moving from Vietnam to Alabama after the Fall of Saigon. (Bonus: this won the National Book Award for Young People's Literature in 2011 and could be used for Challenge #7.)

Papers in the Wind by **Eduardo Sacheri** (South America): A heartwarming and funny novel in which a group of friends attempt to secure the financial future for their dead friend's daughter by selling his share in a minor league soccer player.

On Beauty by **Zadie Smith** (Europe): This uproariously funny, relentlessly provocative novel follows the exploits of multi-racial, intercontinental family (the husband is an Englishman, the wife an African-American) in a fictional college town in New England.

My Brilliant Career by **Miles Franklin** (Australia): A novel about a budding feminist growing up in rural Australia, this classic was first published in 1901, when the author was still a teenager!

TITLE

AUTHOR

PUBLISHER:

YEAR PUBLISHED:

GENRE/SUBJECT:

STARTED

FINISHED

REVIEW:

This book in 3 words

-
-
-

RATING: A   B   C   D   F

NOTES, QUOTES, and other things to remember:

AFTERTHOUGHTS

How did this challenge influence your reading experience?

_____

_____

_____

_____

_____

_____

_____

What insights did you gain from this challenge?

_____

_____

_____

_____

_____

_____

_____

TITLE

AUTHOR

PUBLISHER:

YEAR PUBLISHED:

GENRE/SUBJECT:

STARTED

FINISHED

REVIEW:

This book in 3 words

RATING: A   B   C   D   F

NOTES, QUOTES, and other things to remember:

TITLE

AUTHOR

PUBLISHER:

YEAR PUBLISHED:

GENRE/SUBJECT:

STARTED   **FINISHED**

REVIEW:

This book in 3 words

-
-
-

RATING: **A**   **B**   **C**   **D**   **F**

NOTES, QUOTES, and other things to remember:

_____
_____
_____
_____
_____
_____
_____
_____
_____
_____
_____
_____
_____
_____
_____
_____
_____
_____
_____
_____
_____
_____
_____
_____
_____
_____

TITLE

AUTHOR

PUBLISHER:

YEAR PUBLISHED:

GENRE/SUBJECT:

STARTED

FINISHED

REVIEW:

This book in 3 words

-
-
-

RATING: A   B   C   D   F

NOTES, QUOTES, and other things to remember:

YEARLY GRAPH: Fill in the boxes to track your reading

BOOKS / MONTH 20___

	1	2	3	4	5	6	7	8	9	10	11	12	13	14	15	16	17	18	19	20
JAN																				
FEB																				
MAR																				
APR																				
MAY																				
JUN																				
JUL																				
AUG																				
SEP																				
OCT																				
NOV																				
DEC																				

BOOKS / MONTH 20__

	1	2	3	4	5	6	7	8	9	10	11	12	13	14	15	16	17	18	19	20
JAN																				
FEB																				
MAR																				
APR																				
MAY																				
JUN																				
JUL																				
AUG																				
SEP																				
OCT																				
NOV																				
DEC																				

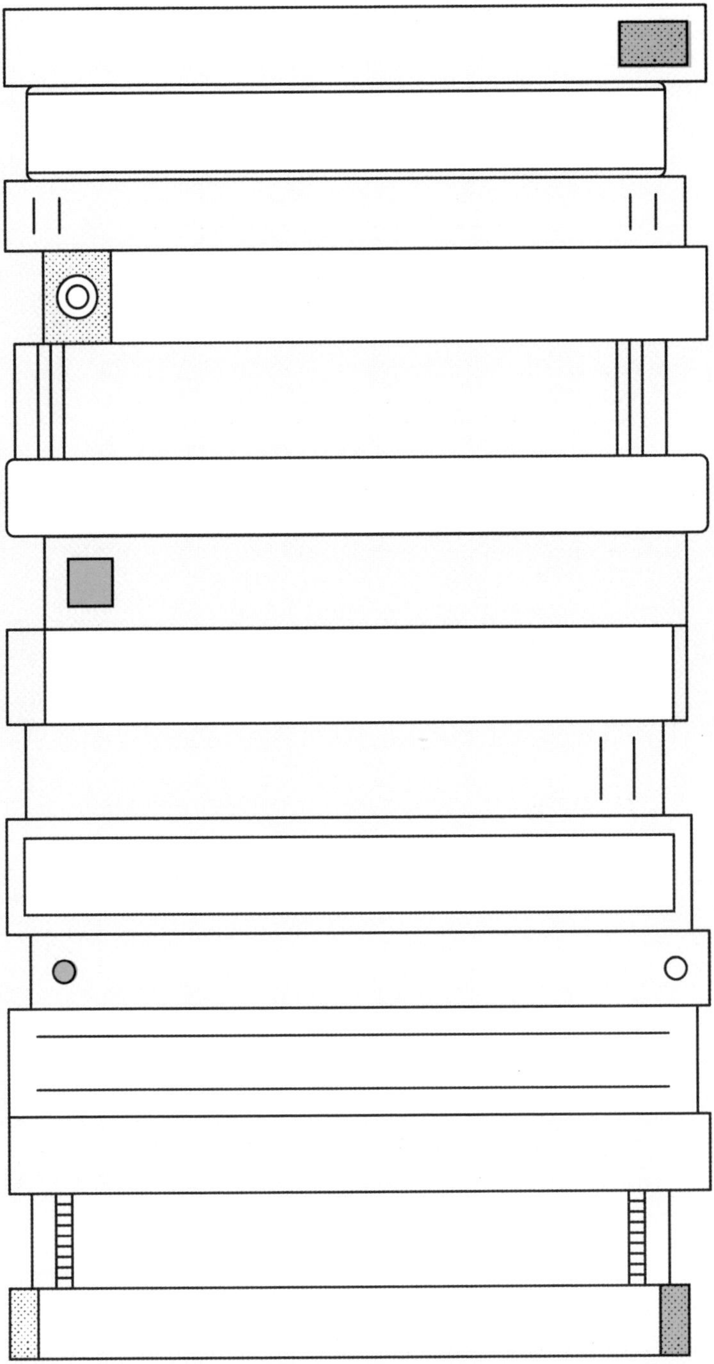

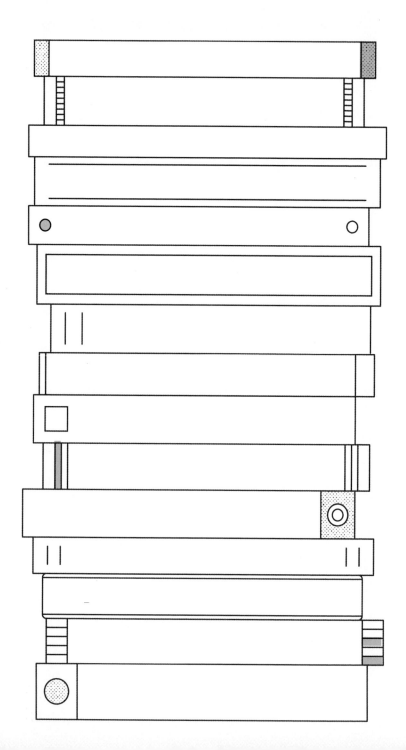